A QUICK & EASY GUIDE TO
SEX & DISABILITY

A. ANDREWS

A QUICK & EASY GUIDE TO SEX & DISABILITY

A. ANDREWS

A LIMERENCE PRESS
PUBLICATION

HEY, THANKS! I want to take a second to say that while I'm proud to say that this book is mine, ultimately it exists because of the many disabled folks doing this work and sharing their experiences with the rest of us. I'm so grateful to those who have spent time and emotional energy in educating me, shared their personal insights and experiences with both me and the world, and influenced my personal framework and understanding of disability sexuality. A special thanks to Carrie Wade: your friendship and wisdom is truly a gift.

Designed by Kate Z. Stone
Edited by Ari Yarwood

Published by Limerence Press, Inc. • Ari Yarwood, founder
Limerence Press is an imprint of Oni-Lion Forge Publishing Group, LLC

JAMES LUCAS JONES, president & publisher • **SARAH GAYDOS**, editor in chief • **CHARLIE CHU**, e.v.p. of creative & business development • **BRAD ROOKS**, director of operations • **AMBER O'NEILL**, special projects manager **HARRIS FISH**, events manager • **MARGOT WOOD**, director of marketing & sales • **JEREMY ATKINS**, director of brand communications • **DEVIN FUNCHES**, sales & marketing manager • **KATIE SAINZ**, marketing manager **TARA LEHMANN**, marketing & publicity associate • **TROY LOOK**, director of design & production • **KATE Z. STONE**, senior graphic designer • **SONJA SYNAK**, graphic designer • **HILARY THOMPSON**, graphic designer • **SARAH ROCKWELL**, junior graphic designer • **ANGIE KNOWLES**, digital prepress lead • **VINCENT KUKUA**, digital prepress technician • **SHAWNA GORE**, senior editor • **ROBIN HERRERA**, senior editor • **AMANDA MEADOWS**, senior editor **JASMINE AMIRI**, editor • **GRACE BORNHOFT**, editor • **ZACK SOTO**, editor • **STEVE ELLIS**, vice president of games **BEN EISNER**, game developer • **MICHELLE NGUYEN**, executive assistant • **JUNG LEE**, logistics coordinator **JOE NOZEMACK**, publisher emeritus

ohheyitsalyssa.com
@alyssashmalyssa

limerencepress.com
@limerencepress

First Edition: May 2020
ISBN: 978-1-62010-694-5
eISBN: 978-1-62010-706-5

Library of Congress Control Number: 2019940880

Printed in Hong Kong.

10 9 8 7 6 5 4 3 2 1

Ahem....
Disabled people have sex!
Trust me, I know.

I know what you're thinking... Who the heck am I?
CUE THE INTRODUCTIONS!
Hey! Hi! Hello! I'm A! A totally queer, totally complete, incomplete paraplegic cartoonist with some pep in my step about changing the ways we talk (and don't talk) about sex and intimacy...
...for all bodies.
Like, all of them.

It's true... I'm no doctor or sex educator.
I'm just a disabled cartoonist.

Well—a disabled cartoonist that has sex!

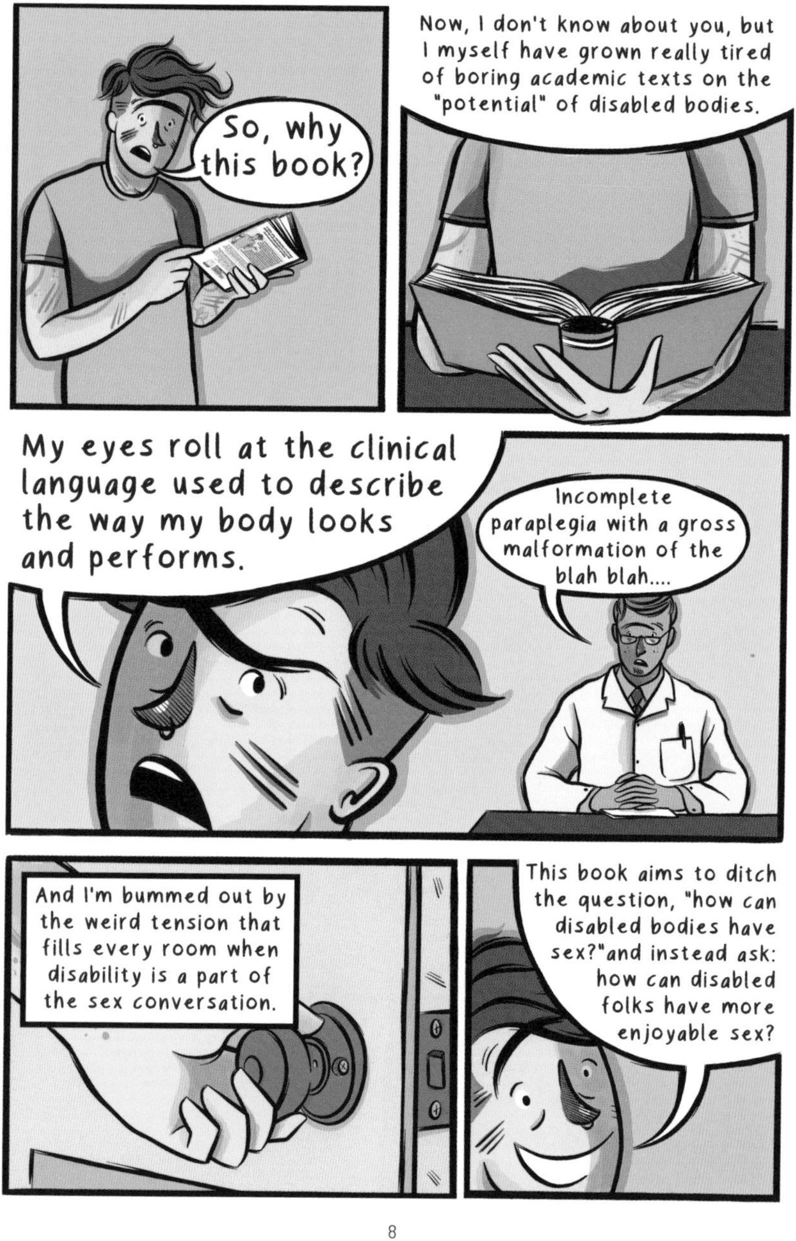
So, why this book?
Now, I don't know about you, but I myself have grown really tired of boring academic texts on the "potential" of disabled bodies.
My eyes roll at the clinical language used to describe the way my body looks and performs.
Incomplete paraplegia with a gross malformation of the blah blah....
And I'm bummed out by the weird tension that fills every room when disability is a part of the sex conversation.
This book aims to ditch the question, "how can disabled bodies have sex?"and instead ask: how can disabled folks have more enjoyable sex?

*According to reports by the CDC, and World Health Organization.

But somehow, despite the boom in social consciousness...
...and the sudden revelation that we are, in fact, out in the wild living our lives...
...disabled folks remain less likely to receive adequate sex education and sexual healthcare, and more likely to experience sexual trauma and heavy stigma surrounding all things S-E-X than our able-bodied peers.*
Ugh. I'm not gonna draw that trash.

*According to the World Health Organization, and Disability Justice.

Sounds pretty bleak....
I know. But it doesn't have to be this way!
Beyond being possible, sex for all bodies can be fun!
So, let's ditch the clinical language, the bummer statistics, and the trash misconceptions, and just talk about it.

DISABILITY SEXUALITY

A quickie before we get to the quickies!
DEFINING DISABILITY
It's not that definitions aren't out there, but disability is hard to define.
Disabilities [noun
difficult for someo
mental, physical,
person's life activ
I'd argue that there's no single definition that feels all-encompassing.
While there are shared impacts within the disability community, disability looks and feels different for everyone.

Apart from differing types of disability...
Congenital Disability: A condition had since birth.
Acquired Disability: Acquired through injury or the onset of illness or disease.
Intellectual Disability: Conditions affecting intellectual ability or mental capacity.
But, you don't look disabled....
Invisible Disability: Chronic illness, mental illness, sensory or spectrum disorders.
...there are various ways our disabilities present (or don't!)...
I have Cerebral Palsy!
Me too!
...various environmental impacts affecting disability...
age
race
class
sexuality
size
gender
ethnicity
faith
...and various intersecting identities impacting disability.

All of these things intersect, shaping our worldviews, our identities, and our experiences of what it means to be disabled.
While this book has handy information for any and all bodies and persons, disabled or not, an important thing to note going forward is that it does focus most heavily on physical accessibility needs and considerations in sex.
All disability presents differently.
They are all valid, real, and have unique needs and considerations.

...let's make sure we're all on the same page, and debunk some...

I didn't want to have to do this, but fine...

MYTHS ABOUT DISABLED BODIES

Disabled people aren't attractive.
EXCUUUUSE ME?!?
Disabled people don't care about things like sex.
I'm literally writing an entire book about it.
This is a book. I made it.
Disabled people can't perform sex.
What I **can't** do is juggle.

Myth or not, however, the things folks say can have an impact on our sense of self-worth.
For those of us who are disabled, establishing and maintaining a positive body image can be a real challenge... ...and I don't have an easy solution.

The thing that sucks the most about the lies we're told about disability and desirability, is that it's not just the able-bodied folks who have to unpack them.
We are also taught those lies—about ourselves.
Yet somehow, despite every myth, every ounce of insecurity, and every message that tells us we shouldn't be, here we are—at a crossroads between "disabled" and "horny."
What do we do?

First, we set the record straight: Disabled people are **HUNKS**! We ditch all of the bad messaging, the misconceptions, and the harsh comparisons. We get to know and love ourselves.
Okay, okay. I get what you're saying and all... ...but, now what?

COMMUNICATION

We need to talk....
No really, though! The key to great sex, for literally everyone, is communication!
Good communication is the big trick to getting it right with everything from your intimate relationships...
...Can I?!?
Yes, please!
...to your Chipotle order!
Oh. My. God. I forgot to add guac!

Communicating your needs, expectations, and anxieties isn't easy—for anyone.
But talking about sex with partners, peers, or health professionals can feel particularly difficult when you're disabled.
Wait, I've got to talk to **all** those people?!
Don't worry. It's not only totally possible, it's worth it.

Disabled or not, the first step to getting down is figuring out what sex even means to you, anyway.
We're taught all kinds of mixed messages about what sex is supposed to be, but all that really matters is what it is to you and your partner or partners.
There is no script, no formula, and no defining act. Just you, your partner, and all the things that make your bodies feel good. You can define sex however you want! And you can change that definition at any time!

In *What You Really Really Want*, Jaclyn Friedman writes that the first person you need to learn to communicate with about sex is yourself...
WHAT YOU REALLY (REALLY) WANT
...and it's true.
So, what do you like?
Um....
It's hard to imagine being able to articulate your boundaries, wants, desires, or concerns with anyone...
...if you haven't really communicated it to yourself.
Fear not! I have some ideas.

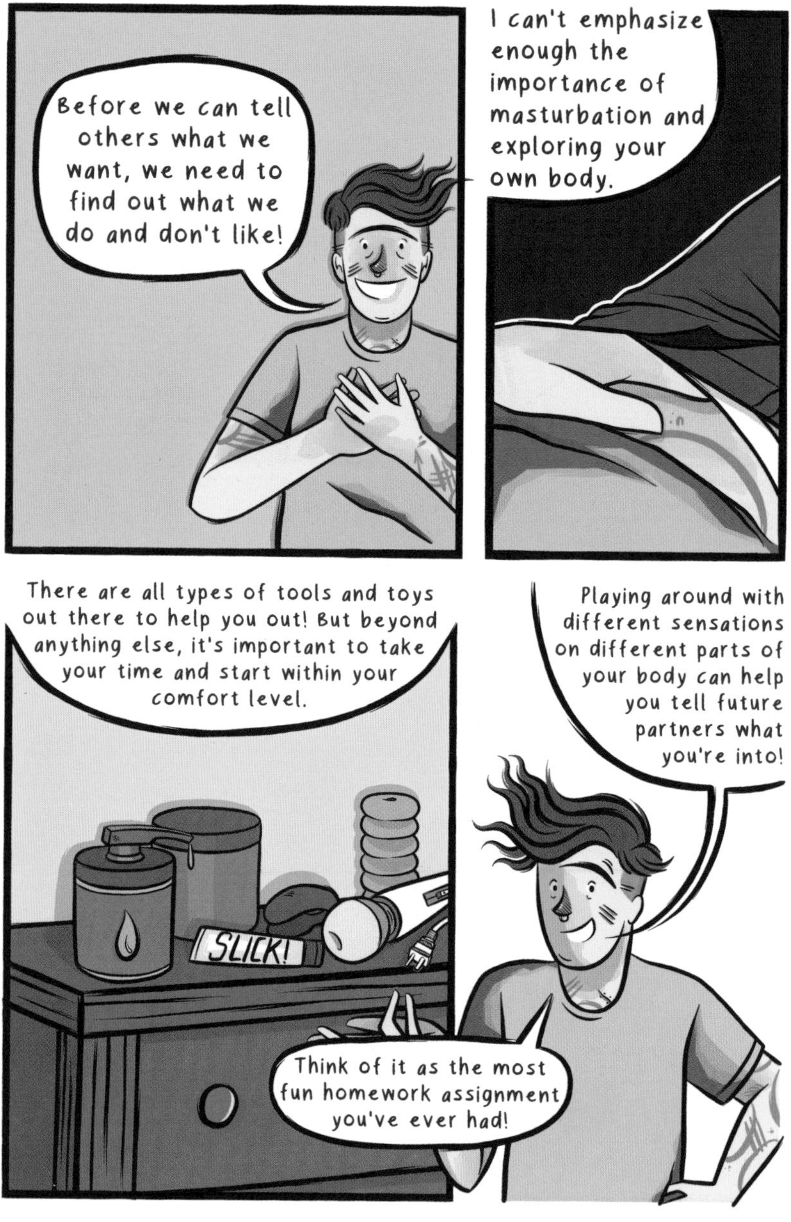
Before we can tell others what we want, we need to find out what we do and don't like!
I can't emphasize enough the importance of masturbation and exploring your own body.
There are all types of tools and toys out there to help you out! But beyond anything else, it's important to take your time and start within your comfort level.
Playing around with different sensations on different parts of your body can help you tell future partners what you're into!
SLICK!
Think of it as the most fun homework assignment you've ever had!

There are a lot of parts of our bodies that we may not be comfortable with...
...focus on what feels good! Pleasure and sex aren't just about genitals.
And when all physical endeavors feel out of reach, don't be afraid to expand your mind! Erotic stories and visual stimulation can help too!

ACTIVITY TIME!

Most often, the hardest thing about communication is figuring out where and how to begin. Here are some prompts to help you out.

Things about sex that make me feel excited:

Things about sex that make me feel anxious:

Parts of my body that I like being touched:

Parts of my body that are off-limits:

Words that I like my body and genitals to be called:

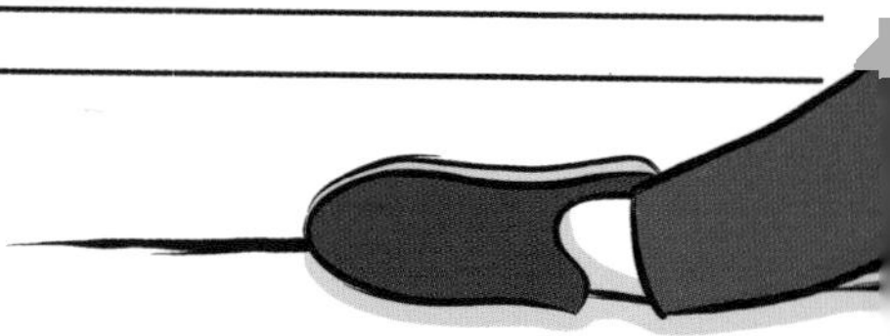

Sexual acts I want to try:

A thing I might need help with:

If the risk feels like it outweighs the reward in communicating your findings with a potential partner, it's not a sign that your wants are too much, but that the partner you're considering just may not be right for you.
If you're feeling rich in rewards, maybe it's worth the share!

Well, this is awkward....
If it all feels a bit silly, that's okay. Sex can be silly.
If it all feels a little overwhelming, that's also okay...
...sex can feel that way too, sometimes.
Communication is a skill. And like any good skill, it takes time and practice.

But, I'm able-bodied. What do I say?
Can you still...? You know....
Not that. Never that.
Oh. Sorry.

It's okay. Finding the right words can be hard. These things happen.
So... what **should** I say?
Try something more like....
What do you like?

Let's workshop a few more communication do's and don'ts.
INSTEAD OF...
TRY THIS...
I don't even notice your disability....
I love your body!
I've never been attracted to a disabled person....
This is all new for me, but I'm excited to learn!

There are a lot of ways "the talk" could play out.
If you're feeling anxious about it, taking it outside of the bedroom can be helpful.
This feels...
...awkward?
Changing up the space and talking it out before you're in the throws of it can ease some of the pressure and help you connect.
I want to talk to you about sex, but I'm feeling a little nervous.
It's okay, take your time!

What if they don't want me? What if I open myself up and they lose interest?
What if my disability turns them off?
What if they say something awful?
What if...?
Hearing "no" is hard. But, though it can be tough...
...learning to cope with rejection is the best communication skill any of us can hope to have.
Some people's reasons will feel like downright garbage.
Some people's reasons will just **be** downright garbage.
But there's no reason required in consent, and whether or not it is nice, a "no" is a "no" all the same.

I know, but how do you deal with it?
When it all feels too hard, it helps to have a...
SELF-CARE PLAN
Reach out to your pals for support!
Here for ya, pal.
"The Decompression Buddy"
Write yourself a love letter for a rainy day!
"The Rejection Mantra"
And when all else fails, give yourself the gift of a good cry! Sometimes things just suck and we've got to let ourselves feel our way through it.
"The Good Ol' Fashioned Cry"

Any and all rejection heckin' sucks, but some people just aren't our people. Knowing who isn't for us just paves way for the folks who will be.
It's cheesy, I know. But it's true!
Should have applied for that Hallmark gig!

Anyway! Cool, so no more talking, right?
WRONG, SUCKER!
Communication is the currency of the world, so beef up those wallets, pals!

Our partners aren't the only people we share our lives with.
For those of us with personal care attendants...
Thanks for talking to me about it! I'm happy to help you in whatever way feels comfortable for both of us and our boundaries.
...it may be helpful to talk to them about your sex life and sexual health needs...
...and how they may coincide with your overall care.
We'll get you all set up here, and you'll be good to go!

And while all disability isn't necessarily medical, being able to talk about your sexual health with your doctor and other health care providers is important too.
Addressing our sexual and reproductive health is a major part of staying healthy in general.
I'm thinking about having sex, and I'd like to talk to you about my birth control options.
And, for some of us with limited sensation, surgical histories, or pain, it can be important to discuss safety and risks of injury to consider.
How long after my procedure should I wait before I can safely have sex again?

Who knew all this boning would require so much talking!
Heck yeah! I know, I know. It sounds like a lot...
...but try not to sweat it too much.
I promise you, the juice is worth the squeeze.

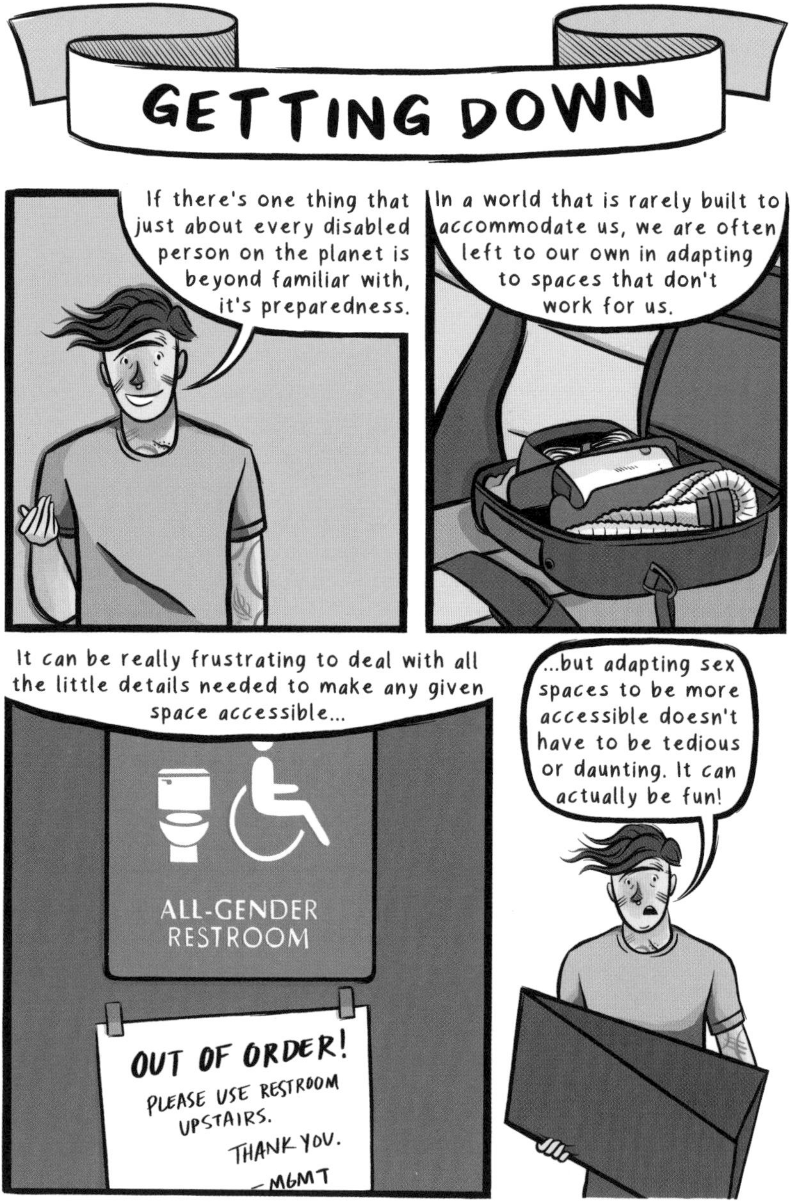
GETTING DOWN
If there's one thing that just about every disabled person on the planet is beyond familiar with, it's preparedness.
In a world that is rarely built to accommodate us, we are often left to our own in adapting to spaces that don't work for us.
It can be really frustrating to deal with all the little details needed to make any given space accessible...
ALL-GENDER RESTROOM
OUT OF ORDER!
PLEASE USE RESTROOM UPSTAIRS.
THANK YOU.
-MGMT
...but adapting sex spaces to be more accessible doesn't have to be tedious or daunting. It can actually be fun!

Making sure that your toys and equipment, positioning furniture, lube, and clean-up supplies (we'll get to all of that) are within reach is a solid start!
Setting the scene for the sex you want helps to ease any anxiety around unwanted interruptions.
It also builds up the anticipation, which can be exciting!

For folks who experience incontinence, equipping your space with waterproof pads or blankets can help with unwanted (or wanted!) messes.
Any mattress pad, waterproof sheet, or blanket can do the trick, but finding an item made for use specifically during play can make the sex space feel less sterile and more sexy...

...all while making for easy and stress-free clean-up!

Bladder and bowel incontinence can be a major source of anxiety for lots of folks.
While sexual stimulation can encourage incontinence...
...there are lots of ways to approach it that can take some of the edge off.
Like talking about it! Finding a little gentle humor! Developing a game plan around it!
Both urinary and fecal incontinence are more common than you might think... for all bodies!
Hey, pal! Sex is weird! And weird is good!
I'm glad we're talking about it. I want you to feel safe.
Knowing that incontinence **may** happen, and communicating your needs around it with your partner, makes for a better overall time!

Honestly, if you finish this book and leave with only one tiny nugget of wisdom, please let it be that of the glory of a good lube.
Everything is better wetter! And that's a fact.
Okay, maybe not everything, but you knew what I meant.
Lube is an absolute must when it comes to safer and more enjoyable sex.

This is especially true when stimulating a part of the body with limited or no sensation, as they may be more prone to injury and irritation.
Lots of bodies have difficulty producing lubrication on their own...
...making lube all the more important!

There's also a variety when it comes to your lubricant options.
GLIDE
And what works for one body (or barrier method)...
...does'n't work for all bodies (or barrier methods)!
It's crucial to find the lube that feels best for you and your partner!
And to apply it generously!

When it comes to barrier methods in sex practices involving a penis, nothing really beats a condom.
(1) CHECK!
(2) PINCH!
(3) ROLL!
A well-fitted condom can be effective in the prevention of pregnancy, HIV, and most sexually transmitted infections.

Some other barrier options:

NITRILE GLOVES
(for hand-to-genital or hand-to-anus contact)

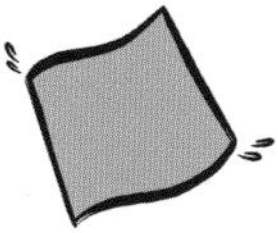

DENTAL DAMS
(for mouth-to-genital or mouth-to-anus contact)

FC2 CONDOM
(an insertable vaginal condom option)

Always be sure your lube is compatible with the barrier you're using, and be mindful of potential sensitivities to frequently used materials such as latex.
And though they exist, it's best to stay clear of barriers with added flavoring or spermicides as they can cause irritation.

Nobody wants that!

POSITIONING

There are an infinite number of ways for two (or more!) bodies to connect.
No two bodies are the exact same...
...and the ways we go about fitting them together doesn't need to be either!
Getting creative with your positioning not only makes for more comfortable sex... it's also just hot!

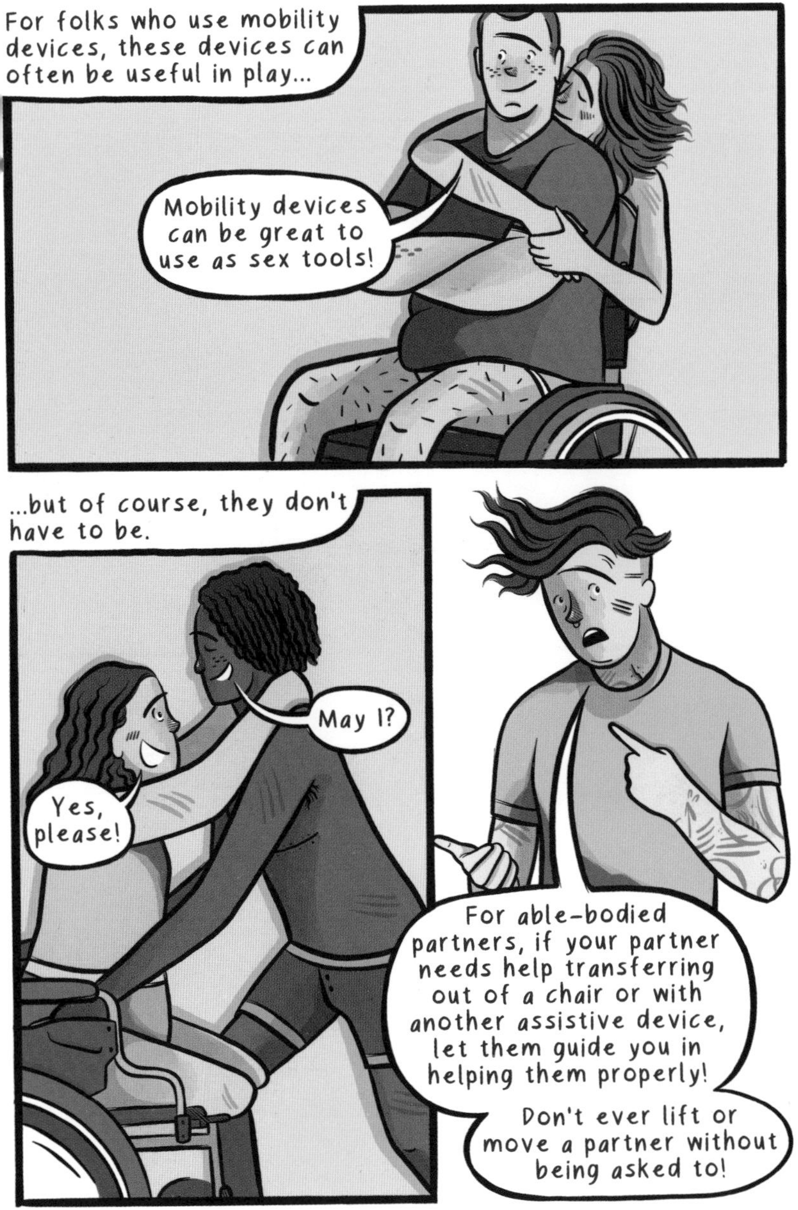
For folks who use mobility devices, these devices can often be useful in play...
Mobility devices can be great to use as sex tools!
...but of course, they don't have to be.
May I?
Yes, please!
For able-bodied partners, if your partner needs help transferring out of a chair or with another assistive device, let them guide you in helping them properly!
Don't ever lift or move a partner without being asked to!

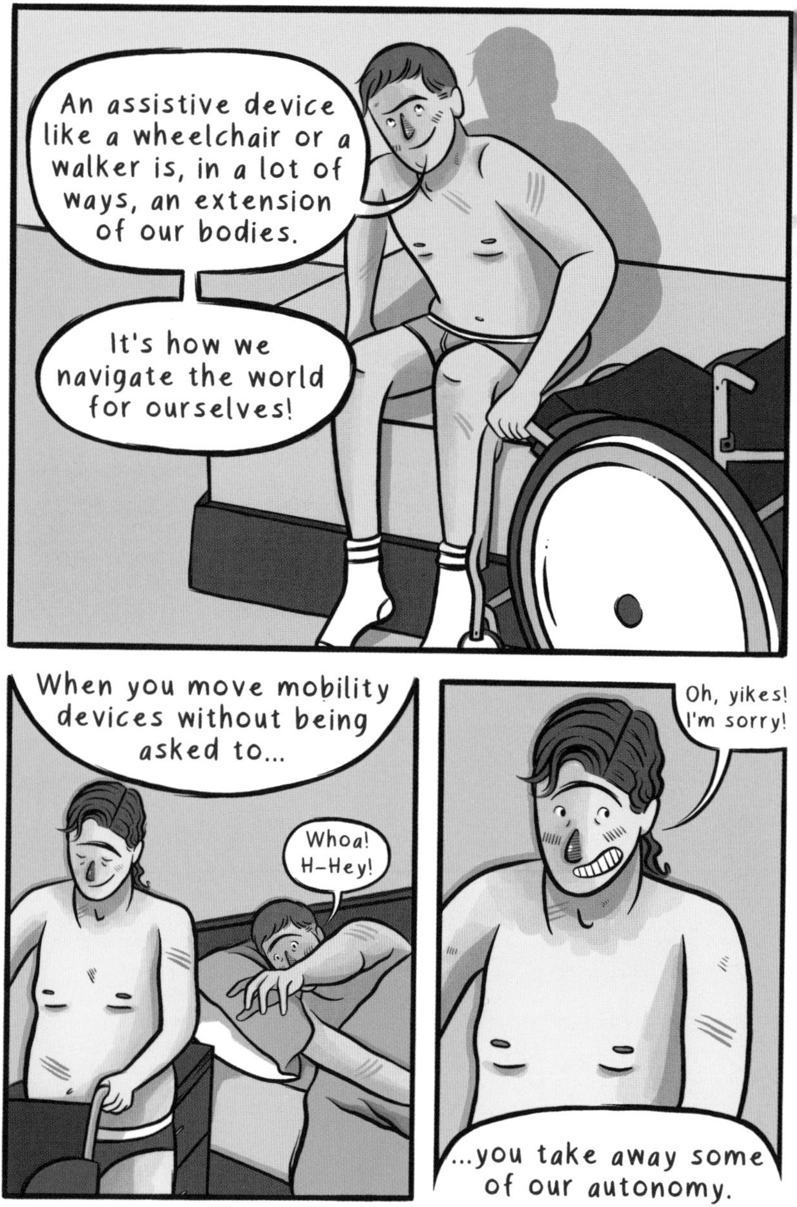
An assistive device like a wheelchair or a walker is, in a lot of ways, an extension of our bodies.
It's how we navigate the world for ourselves!
When you move mobility devices without being asked to...
Whoa! H-Hey!
Oh, yikes! I'm sorry!
...you take away some of our autonomy.

The ways we choose to position our bodies can affect everything from our body's reaction to stimulation...
...to our general feelings of comfort and safety.
And when it comes to accessible sex positioning, props are your pals!

There is a wide variety of positioning furniture made specifically for comfortability during play:

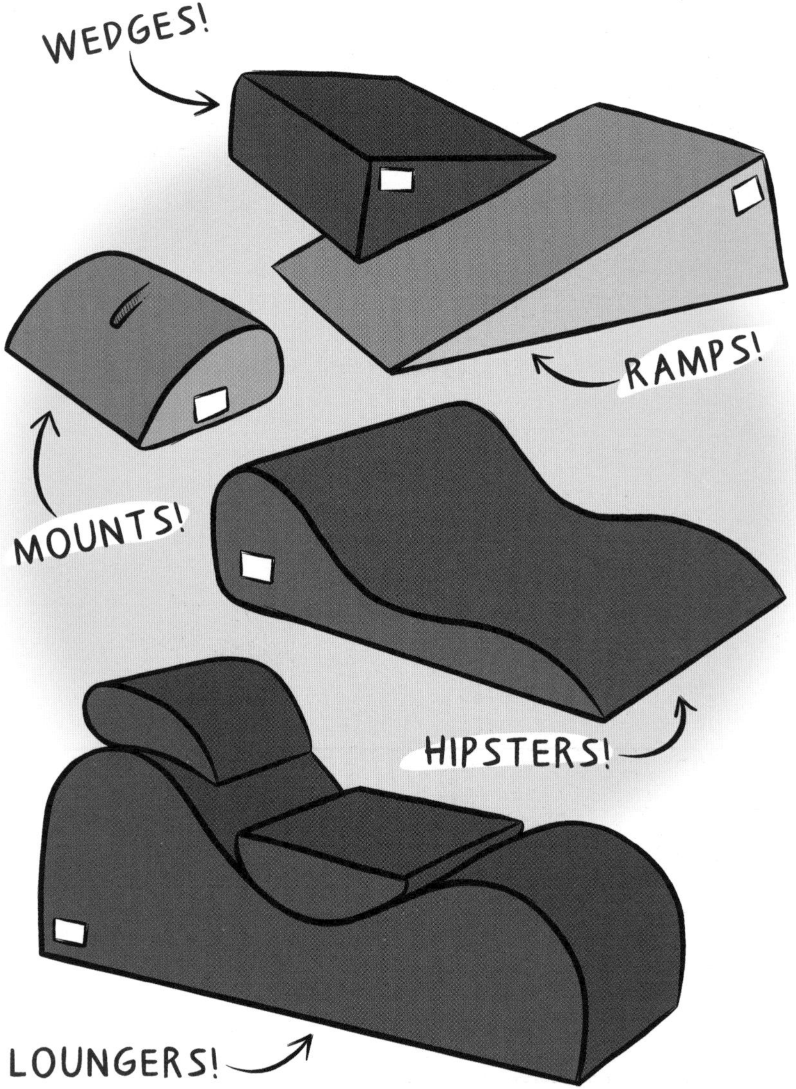

Getting creative with your positioning can be useful for size differences between bodies...
...easing joints and muscles for those with chronic pain...
...and achieving stimulation in areas that may otherwise be hard to reach!
And honestly? There are enough things to stress over reaching for. A good time shouldn't be one!

Now, it's about time we all get on the same page...
...about sex toys!
And break down some of the myths about them!
Shouldn't I be able to do it myself?
Why, though?!
Doesn't it kind of ruin the intimacy?
No way, pal!
Isn't that, y'know... kinky? I don't think I want that.

No matter the sex you're into, sex toys can be fun for anyone!
Think of them as really handy access tools!

Is that better?!
Yes!

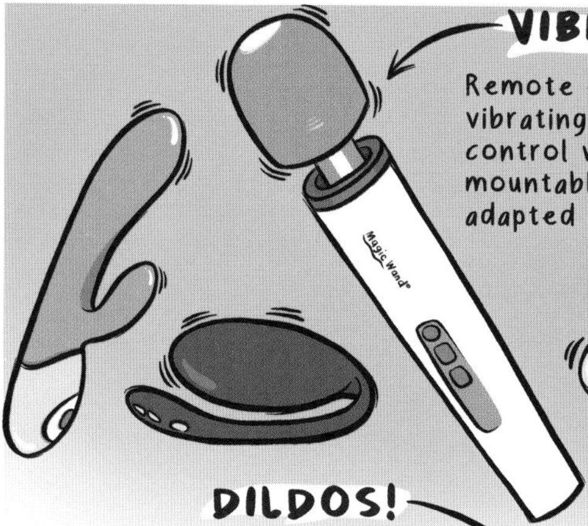

VIBES!

Remote or app-controlled vibrating toys help keep control within reach, and mountable toys can be adapted for hands-free play!

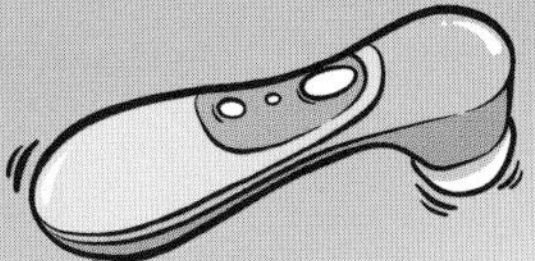

DILDOS!

Dildos and extenders come in a lot of sizes for folks with vaginas or penises of varying functionality.

PLUGS & BEADS!

For those interested in anal play, there are a variety of toys with flared bases safe for anal penetration. Plugs with a more slender base are best for seated wear.

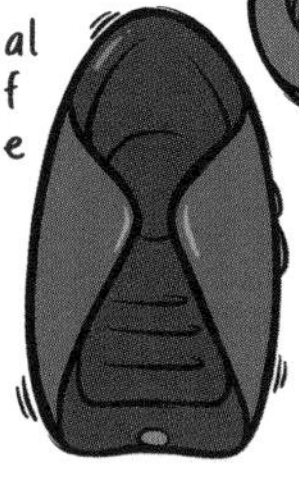

RINGS!

Cock rings can enhance sensation for the wearer or the receiving partner in penetrative play. Vibrating options can provide app or remote-controlled access.

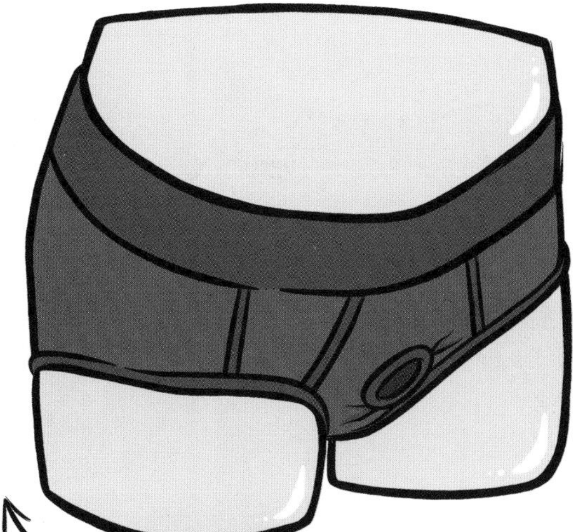

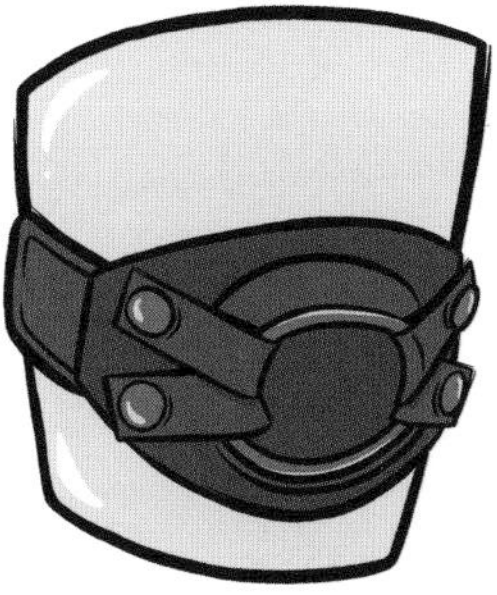

HARNESSES!

From gloved options to thigh straps, there are a variety of harness styles that can benefit folks with hip spasticity, joint pain, or muscle weakness.

The weight and grip of the toys you choose can make all the difference when it comes to muscle and joint pain.
And for additional positioning support, there are various swings and slings to help you out!

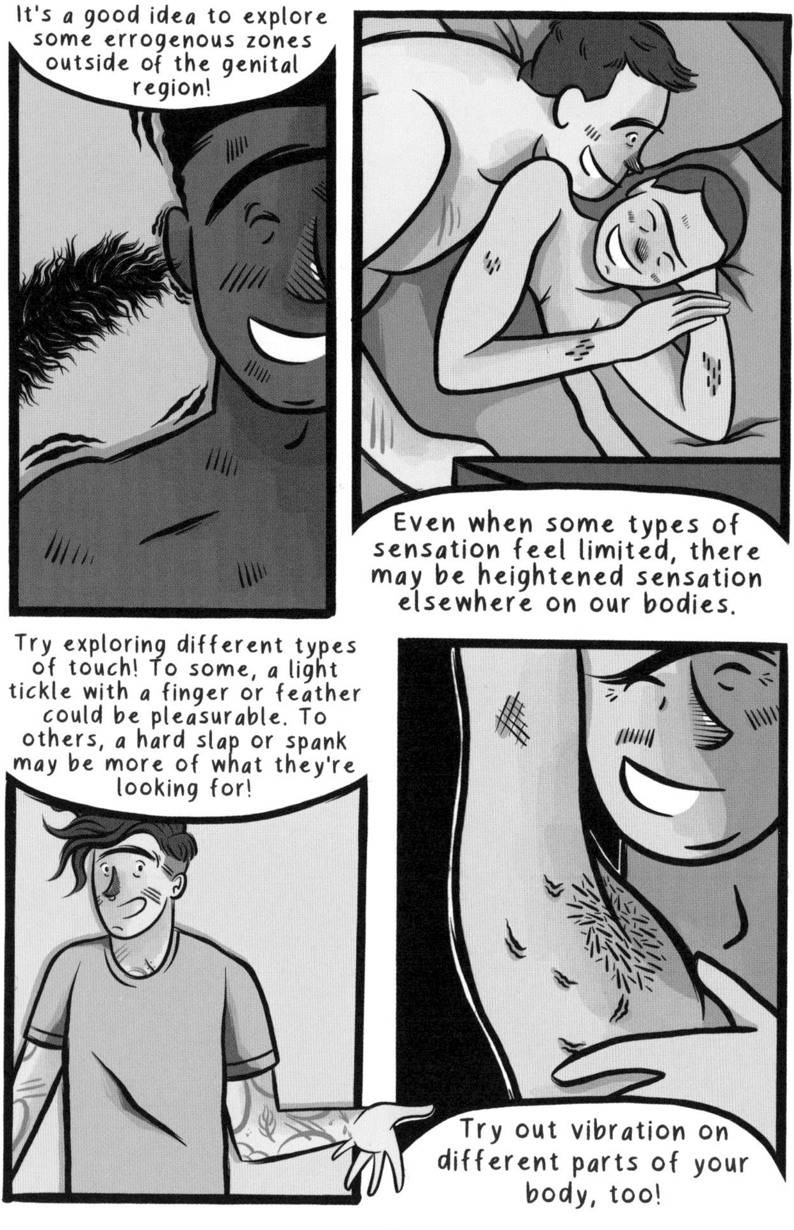
It's a good idea to explore some errogenous zones outside of the genital region!
Even when some types of sensation feel limited, there may be heightened sensation elsewhere on our bodies.
Try exploring different types of touch! To some, a light tickle with a finger or feather could be pleasurable. To others, a hard slap or spank may be more of what they're looking for!
Try out vibration on different parts of your body, too!

With a balance of communication and creativity, sex really can be anything and everything you want it to be.
CRASH!
Even it it's a little fumbly and silly from time to time.
Especially if it's a little fumbly and silly from time to time!

I know that I can't cover everything...
A QUICK & EASY GU TO SEX & DISABIL
A. ANDREWS
...it's a **quick** and **easy** guide!
But there are a few specifics we should chat about!

Let's talk... SPASTICITY!
For some bodies, sexual stimulation can bring on involuntary spasms...
...which can cause a bit of a challenge.
As a result, penetrative sex can be painful and some folks may choose to avoid it in their play.
That's okay! There are lots of other things we can do!
But some may find spasticity can lessen after an orgasm (an involuntary autonomic nervous response resulting in a pleasure-filled climax) making penetration more enjoyable.
So penetration isn't off the table, but it's something that may take a little working up to!
Soaking in baths and other calming activities can also be helpful!

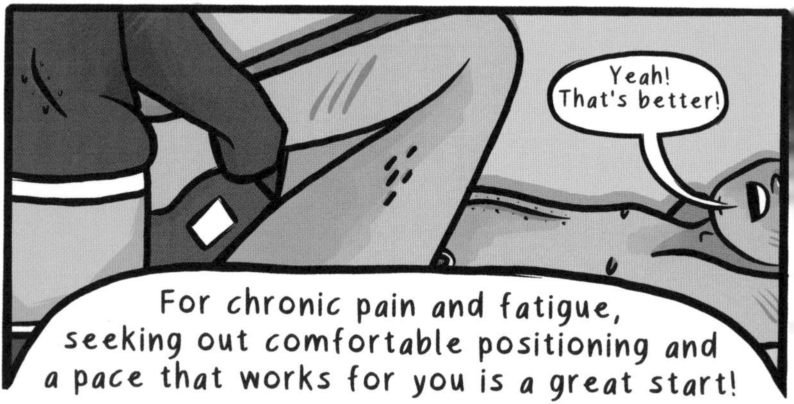
Yeah! That's better!
For chronic pain and fatigue, seeking out comfortable positioning and a pace that works for you is a great start!

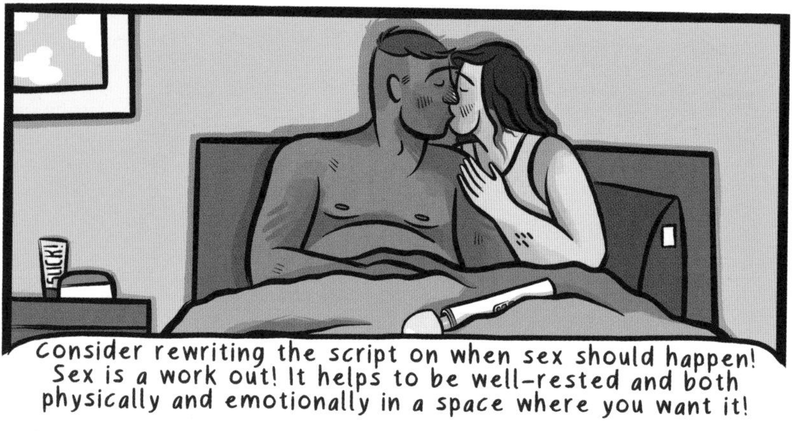
SLICK!
Consider rewriting the script on when sex should happen! Sex is a work out! It helps to be well-rested and both physically and emotionally in a space where you want it!

And it's never a bad idea to take breaks! I can assure you it doesn't ruin any moods.

And while it's true that having a disability doesn't take away our sexuality...
...some disabilities and chronic illnesses do have unique considerations that may make certain types of play unsafe or unenjoyable.
Listening to your body is important, even when limitations feel stifling.
Are you okay?
Sorry. It's just not working for me right now.
Remember that talking to your partner about the things that don't work for you opens you both up to finding other things that will!
That's okay! We could always try something else!

AFTERCARE
Emotionally speaking...
...the most important piece of any and all sexual activity is AFTERCARE.
Isn't that like—a BDSM thing?
Well, yeah. But...
...it's really just an everybody thing!

Whether the sex you're having is romantic or casual...
...it's important to check in and get (and give!) the emotional support and care that you need afterward.
How are you feeling?
Sex can evoke all kinds of unforeseeable feelings and emotions even when we have established boundaries with one another...
CHECK! IN!

Talk to your partner about what might feel good for you after sex!

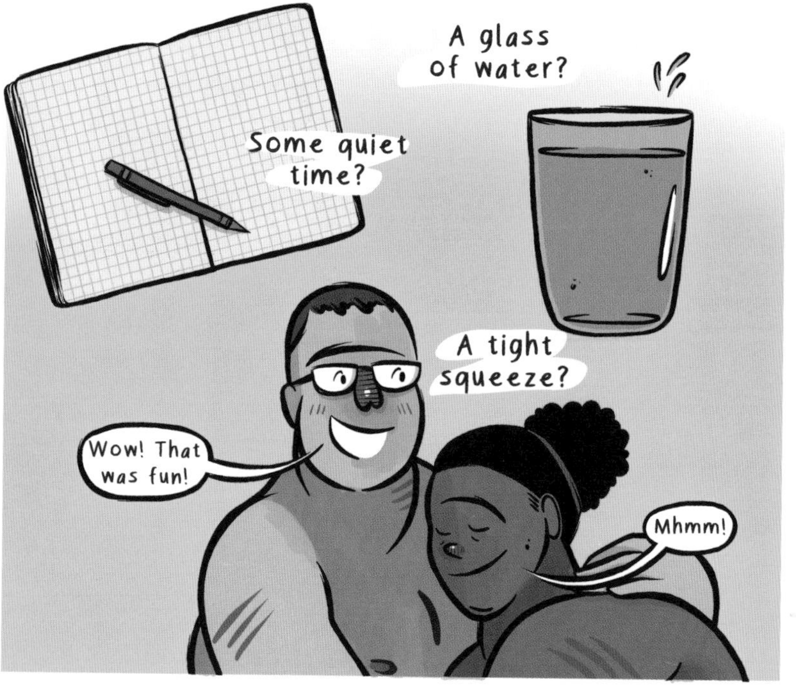
A glass of water?
Some quiet time?
A tight squeeze?
Wow! That was fun!
Mhmm!

Know that sometimes, despite doing it all by the book, sex can make us feel not-so-great...
...for seemingly no reason at all.
Sex therapists and other care professionals are always a good option when you need a bit of help working it all out.

When it comes down to it, sex is whatever the heck you want it to be! And with the right tools, communication, and comfort in yourself and your sexuality, the possibilities are endless!

So, go out there and get laid, pals!
(If you wanna!)

For more information, check out these cool additional resources!

PRINT

The Ultimate Guide to Sex and Disability: For All of Us Who Live with Disabilities, Chronic Pain, and Illness —Miriam Kaufman, Cory Silverberg, & Fran Odette

What You Really, Really Want: The Smart Girl's Shame-Free Guide to Sex and Safety—Jaclyn Friedman

Sex and Disability—Robert McRuer & Anna Mollow

Exile and Pride: Disability, Queerness, and Liberation —Eli Clare

Kissability: People with Disabilities Talk About Sex, Love, and Relationships—Katherine Duke

QDA: A Queer Disability Anthology—Raymond Luczak

PODCASTS

Disability After Dark—Andrew Gurza

Disability Visibility Project—Alice Wong

WEB

Crutches and Spice—Imani Barbarin

Squirmy and Grubs—Shane Burcaw & Hannah Aylward

Autostraddle

A. ANDREWS

is a queer and disabled cartoonist living and working in Minneapolis, Minnesota after a near-decade stay in New York City. They grew up in the Pacific Northwest sketching in hospitals, and are the creator of the Autostraddle webcomic *Oh, Hey! It's Alyssa!* When they're not drawing their guts out, they are hanging out with their dog, George, and drinking too many coffees.
